The two Anglo-Saxoɪ of Glouceste

by
Michael Hare

In the course of this lecture I intend to survey the documentary evidence for the ecclesiastical history of Gloucester in the Anglo-Saxon period. The main concern of such a study must be the two minster churches of the town. I shall refer to these two establishments as the old minster and the new minster. That is the terminology which was used in the 10th and 11th centuries, the period with which I shall be principally concerned. The terminology is necessary to avoid confusion, for at this period both houses were dedicated to St Peter[1]. The old minster was the forerunner of the great Benedictine abbey of St Peter, the building of which survives as Gloucester Cathedral. The new minster became the insignificant Augustinian priory of St Oswald, which now survives as a single ruined wall. As we shall see, the different fates of the two houses in the medieval period were largely determined by the time of the Norman Conquest.

I

The old minster was founded about the year 679. The history of the house until the middle of the 9th century has been the subject of an analysis by the late Professor Finberg[2], and I intend to deal fairly briefly with this early period. Finberg showed that the surviving materials were deeply flawed, but that a few basic conclusions can be reached.

The old minster was founded by Osric, a sub-king of the Hwicce. At the time of its foundation it was a double minster, that is to say a house of both men and women ruled by an abbess. The names of the first three abbesses, Cyneburg, Eadburg and Eafe are preserved. The Gloucester *Historia,* a chronicle composed about 1400, states in a muddled passage, that regular life ceased after the death of the last abbess in 767[3]. As Finberg showed this statement is hard to reconcile with the surviving list of benefactions and with independent evidence for the continued existence of a community at Gloucester. That independent evidence comes in the form of the will of Æthelric dated 804[4], preserved at Worcester, which was discussed in detail in last year's lecture[5]. For our purposes what is important is that Æthelric bequeathed an estate of 30 hides at Over to the old minster at Gloucester. Æthelric's will does in fact contain the only reference to the old minster at Gloucester which is found outside its own archives before the 1030s. This reference is particularly valuable for it occurs precisely at the period when we might otherwise infer from the *Historia* that religious life at the old minster had been abandoned, a point to which we will have occasion to return.

We can say almost nothing of the architectural history of the old minster in this early period, except the tradition, recorded in the *Historia*, that Osric and Cyneburg were buried 'before the altar of St Petronilla on the northern side of the monastery'. Even this information must be regarded as suspect, for the cult of St Petronilla, an eponymous daughter of St Peter, only came to prominence in Rome itself in the second half of the 8th century and in the 9th century. It is likely that the *Historia* is describing a much later arrangement[6].

In the first two centuries of its existence, the old minster amassed a huge estate, much of which it preserved through to the time of Domesday Book and later. The list of benefactors reads almost like a roll-call of the rulers of the Hwicce and of the kings of Mercia, and takes us down to the reign of King Burgred of Mercia (852-874). After Burgred we hear almost nothing of the history of the old minster for a century and a half; the next secure date in the history of the establishment is 1022.

II

It is with the middle of the 9th century that my detailed discussion of Gloucester's ecclesiastical history begins. By any standards the middle of the 9th century was a desperate period in English history[7]. Educational standards were ruinous; we may recall King Alfred's comment that when he came to the throne 'so completely had learning decayed in England that there were very few men this side of the Humber who could apprehend their services in English or even translate a letter from Latin into English, and I think that there were not many beyond the Humber'. One of the few surviving pockets of learning, indeed probably the principal such pocket, was at Worcester.

The middle of the 9th century not only saw a decline in educational standards, it also saw the arrival of substantial Viking armies. In the 860s and 870s the ancient kingdom of Mercia collapsed under Viking attack; by 874 the Vikings were able to force King Burgred into exile in Rome. In his place the Danish army appointed one of Burgred's thegns, Ceolwulf, as king and in 877 the Vikings settled in much of eastern and central Mercia.

Ceolwulf was the last king of Mercia. We do not know how his rule came to an end, but by 883 Mercia was governed by an ealdorman, Æthelred, who recognised the overlordship of King Alfred of Wessex (871-899). These events may be part of the aftermath of Alfred's victory over the Vikings at the battle of Edington in 878. Æthelred married Alfred's daughter, Æthelflæd, later in the 880s, and Æthelred and Æthelflæd governed Mercia together until Æthelred's death in 911. Æthelflæd then ruled Mercia alone until her own death in 918; the period of her rule saw the systematic conquest of the eastern Danelaw in conjunction with her brother, Edward the Elder, King of Wessex.

The territory which Æthelred and Æthelflæd governed at the outset of their rule was much smaller than the ancient kingdom of Mercia; they ruled the southern and western parts of the former kingdom. In this shrunken Mercia, Gloucester played a role of special importance; indeed one scholar has called it Æthelred and Æthelflæd's capital[8].

A major aspect of the policy of Alfred in Wessex and of Æthelred and Æthelflæd in Mercia was the construction of fortresses or *burhs;* these *burhs* served initially as places of defence and refuge against the Vikings, and became an offensive tool in the programme of conquest. Gloucester was certainly such a *burh* by the year 914 and probably had been since the early years of the reign of Æthelred and Æthelflæd.

Hand in hand with the provision of fortresses went the renewal of religious life. At Worcester, which Æthelred and Æthelflæd also fortified, this link is made explicit in a surviving charter[9]. Æthelred and Æthelflæd 'ordered the borough to be built at Worcester for the protection of all the people, and also to exalt the praise of God therein'. However the principal religious establishment patronised by Æthelred and Æthelflæd was the new minster which they established at Gloucester, which was to be their burial church.

Our sources for the foundation of the new minster at Gloucester are sadly late. The principal source of evidence is William of Malmesbury, writing in the 1120s. William says that Æthelred and Æthelflæd founded the house in the time of King Alfred[10]; if William's words are taken at face value, the foundation must lie between the mid-880s and 899, the year of Alfred's death. It may be a mistake to place too literal a meaning on William's words, but broad confirmation exists in an extract from a charter of King Athelstan (discussed below), which ascribes the foundation to Æthelred, *primicerius* of the Mericans. A foundation date close to the year 900 seems assured.

The exact purpose of Æthelred and of Æthelflæd in founding a new minster is hard to establish. Their foundation does of course find a close parallel at Winchester where Æthelflæd's brother, Edward the Elder, established the New Minster alongside the Old Minster in about 901[11]. If William of Malmesbury's words are taken at face value, then the Gloucester new minster is earlier than the New Minster at Winchester; it is possible that developments at Gloucester influenced those at Winchester. But even at Winchester, where the documentation is incomparably better than at Gloucester, it is hard to establish Edward's exact purpose. It would be a mistake to press the clear parallels between Gloucester and Winchester too far. The New Minster at Winchester was a great basilican church based on continental models; the new minster at Gloucester was a small and conservative building. At Winchester the New Minster was sited beside the Old Minster in the heart of the Anglo-Saxon *burh* ; at Gloucester the new minster seems on present knowledge to have been peripherally sited.

The choice of site for the new minster is puzzling. It was established on the banks of the Severn away from the walled Roman town (Fig 1); its site may have borne some relationship to the royal palace at Kingsholm[12], which certainly existed in the middle of the 11th century. It seems very curious that the new minster was sited immediately beside one of England's great estuaries during the first Viking age. It is unlikely that it was entirely undefended, but we know as yet nothing of the nature of the defences; it is possible that the principal form of defence was a fortified bridgework across the Severn similar to those which are known to have been established as a defence against the Vikings in mid-9th century France. However that is speculative, and the topographical problem stresses how little we still know about the development of early medieval Gloucester.

The new minster certainly had a pastoral role, for in later centuries St Oswald's had a substantial but entirely extra-mural parish. This parish included the site of the palace at Kingsholm.

It is also possible that the new minster had an educational role. I have already touched on the decay of literature and learning in mid-9th century England. Under King Alfred a systematic educational programme was instituted in Wessex; one of the first measures which Alfred took was the introduction of four scholars from Mercia[13]. One of these four scholars was Werferth, bishop of Worcester, and it is a fair bet that some or even all of the other three came from Worcester, which, as already mentioned, is likely to have been the principal surviving pocket of Latin learning at this period.

In Wessex the progress of Alfred's educational reform is reasonably well documented and has been much elucidated by recent scholarship[14]. Much less is known about Mercia at this time, but it is not unlikely that Æthelred and Æthelflæd shared Alfred's interests. William of Malmesbury, writing in the 12th century, said that Alfred's grandson, the future King Athelstan, was fostered at the court of Æthelred and Æthelflæd[15]; this statement has been doubted but confirmation exists in a source ultimately of Gloucester origin which refers to a 'pact of paternal piety' between Athelstan and Æthelred (see below). Given the educational interests of Alfred's court, it seems to me implicit in this fact that there are also likely to have been reasonable educational facilities at the court of Æthelred and Æthelflæd. It is not improbable that they maintained a school as part of their household just as Alfred did.

Bishop Werferth of Worcester, who played such a prominent part in Alfred's educational revival, is also likely to have played a major role in the affairs of Æthelred and of Æthelflæd. His long episcopate, from 872 to 915, covered almost the entire period of their rule, and we have explicit testimony to his good relations with Æthelred and with Æthelflæd for he is described in one English-language charter as 'their friend'[16].

It is perhaps also worth asking why a new minster was necessary at Gloucester and what role it was to play which could not be undertaken by the old minster. Such little material as we have from the old minster in the mid-9th century displays the characteristic degenerate latinity of the period[17]. It would seem that the old minster was ill-equipped to play a role in fostering a programme of educational reform.

These considerations make it an attractive hypothesis that one of the roles envisaged for the new minster at Gloucester was educational. However, in the absence of both books and documents from the new minster this possibility must remain no more than speculation in the present state of knowledge. We may however look ahead with interest to the fact that our earliest reference to schools in Gloucester is a confirmation by Henry I (1100-35) to St Oswald's of all the schools of Gloucester *(scolas tocius Gloucestrie)*[18].

At the time of its foundation the new minster was dedicated to St Peter, like the old minster. Before long the new minster did however come to be identified with a different saint, Oswald king and martyr (634-642). Oswald was one of the great royal saints of Anglo-Saxon England, and his cult had been made famous in the pages of the Venerable Bede. A substantial part of Oswald's relics made their way to Bardney in the Lincolnshire fens. At Bardney Oswald's shrine was under Mercian tutelage for the best part of 200 years from the late 7th century; his shrine there was honoured by King Offa of Mercia in the second half of the 8th century.

However, by the early 10th century Bardney was under Danish control. In 909 a combined army of West Saxons and Mercians raided the Danelaw, and returned with Oswald's relics which were translated into the new minster at Gloucester. This translation of Oswald's relics can be viewed on more than one level. It was undoubtedly a simple act of piety, but at another level it will have had the symbolic force of legitimising the rule of Æthelred and of Æthelflæd. Oswald's relics would also have been seen as providing protection for the town of Gloucester. The translation of Oswald to Gloucester can be paralleled by other translations to *burhs* established by Æthelred and Æthelflæd, for instance the translation of St Werburg to Chester[19]. The importance to Æthelred and Æthelflæd of their new minster at Gloucester is further demonstrated by their burial there, no doubt in close proximity to Oswald's relics.

Æthelred died in 911 and Æthelflæd in 918. After Æthelflæd's death the kings of Wessex took over direct control of Mercia. However, there is one further additional testimony from the early history of the new minster. That is the record of a charter of King Athelstan in favour of the establishment dated 925 or 926. Although we have no more than an extract from a late source, it bears all the hallmarks of an authentic charter of the period[20]. It is entirely consistent with what we know of Athelstan that he should have issued a charter in favour of the new minster at Gloucester early in his reign. Athelstan is likely to have become familiar with Gloucester and its new minster during the period in his childhood when he was fostered by Æthelred and Æthelflæd, and it is his charter which refers to a 'pact of paternal piety' between Athelstan and Æthelred. Athelstan was moreover an enthusiast for the cult of relics, almost to the point of mania, and the cult of Oswald will no doubt have been important to him[21]. This charter thus provides an important testimony to the patronage of the West Saxon dynasty in the early years after the West Saxon kings assumed direct control of Mercia.

To summarize thus far, we can point to five events in the period of a generation or so in the early history of the new minster. First in about 900 or a little earlier the foundation; secondly the translation of Oswald's relics in 909; thirdly Æthelred's burial in 911; fourthly Æthelflæd's burial in 918 and lastly Athelstan's charter issued in 925 or 926.

III

However, after this early period we have no hard information about the new minster for a little over a century; all that we have are a few incidental references to the presence of Oswald's relics at Gloucester[22]. We next have reliable information about the new minster in the 1030s. Similarly we know nothing about the old minster from the mid-9th century until the 1020s. It is worth speculating on the reasons why we know so little about Gloucester's ecclesiastical history for much of the 10th and early 11th century. I think that we can point to one major factor. In the 7th, 8th and for much of the 9th century, Gloucester was a place of considerable significance to the rulers of the Hwicce and to the kings of Mercia; at the end of the 9th century and in the early 10th century, Gloucester was of central importance to Æthelred and Æthelflæd. Almost all that we know of Gloucester's ecclesiastical history up to the early 10th century can be explained in terms of royal patronage; we learn of royal foundations, royal benefactions, royal burials and a royal translation of royal relics.

The pattern of royal patronage continued at least under Athelstan, as we have seen; in fact Athelstan died at Gloucester in 939, though he was buried at Malmesbury. But the pattern seems to have changed after Athelstan's death. The West Saxon dynasty now ruled the whole of England. Gloucester remained an important regional centre, but it no longer enjoyed centre stage in the preoccupations of the English kings. Gloucester is barely found in the itinerary of English kings in the century after Athelstan's death, though that may in part reflect the predominantly West Saxon bias of our sources. The argument from silence must be used cautiously, but for the later 10th and early 11th century, I think that we can fairly conclude that there was a reduction in the level of active royal patronage towards the two minsters of Gloucester.

The second half of the 10th century was of course anything but a period of silence in the ecclesiastical life of England. The revival of church life, which began under Alfred and which was fostered by his descendants, flowered in the Benedictine reform of English church life. The progress of that reform as it affected individual houses still needs much detailed study. In last year's lecture you heard how precarious was the evidence that there had ever been a monastic reform at Deerhurst[23]. In this lecture I will be discussing the Benedictine reform in relation to both Gloucester minsters. When we come to consider the old minster, we shall see that the main problem to be considered is the date at which the reform took place. In the case of the new minster, the problem is whether it was a reformed Benedictine monastery at any stage of its history. When we first have reliable information, in the post-Conquest period, the new minster was a house of secular canons.

However, the 12th century historian, William of Malmesbury, seems to have been in no doubt that the new minster had once been a proper coenobitic establishment. After describing the foundation of the new minster, William wrote, 'That monastery *(cenobium)* flourished until the time of the Danes and was closely connected to our own house, that is Malmesbury, as may be seen in the muniments of each church', and he adds that the monks were dispersed through the force of hostility and replaced by canons[24]. We do not know what sort of documents led William to these conclusions, though a confraternity agreement might explain the connection with Malmesbury. William does not specifically state that the house was reformed during the second half of the 10th century. It is perfectly possible that he read past history in the language of his own day; in the 12th century monastic and secular religion were distinguished in much more formal terms than in the 10th century. Moreover William knew nothing of the history of the Gloucester old minster in the Anglo-Saxon period; he believed that the old minster was founded by Bishop Ealdred during the reign of Edward the Confessor. On the other hand he seems to have been aware that the original dedication of the new minster was to St Peter. Thus William might mistakenly have interpreted documents from the Anglo-Saxon period relating to the church of St Peter, Gloucester or even to the 'old minster at Gloucester' as referring to the new minster. Moreover, the pre-Conquest Malmesbury archives were themselves far from satisfactory. There are therefore grounds for treating with some caution the words of William of Malmesbury.

There is one other relevant document which needs to be considered. A lease dated 1022 in the old minster archives[25] includes in its witness list 'Anna abbot and all the brothers' of the new minster. I shall argue later that this lease is basically authentic but that it has been translated from Old English into Latin. In the process of translation and copying one sentence was almost certainly misplaced, and in such processes it was also not uncommon for the order of witnesses to be wrongly copied[26]. There is thus no compulsion to take Anna the abbot and the brothers of the new minster together.

In the present state of knowledge there can be no certainty in the matter. It is possible that there was a short-lived period of reformed Benedictine life at the new minster in the late 10th and early 11th century. However it is perhaps more probable that the new minster was never reformed, and that the fact that it was not reformed is itself one of the reasons why the house was later an insignificant foundation.

By the year 1033 the lands of the new minster were being used to endow a foreign clerk at King Cnut's court. So William of Malmesbury's belief that the house underwent a change of fortune in 'the time of the Danes' seems justified. The 'time of the Danes' is a vague phrase; it could apply to the renewed Viking invasions of the late 10th and early 11th centuries or to the subsequent rule by the Danish King Cnut (1016-1035). We can do no more than guess at the causes of the demise of the new minster. I have already discussed the question of the Benedictine reform, certainly likely to have ben a factor in the equation. Another possibility is that the claims of the new minster to the relics of St Oswald were not universally accepted. The dismemberment of Oswald's body on the battlefield led to a great proliferation of his relics, and Gloucester's claims may have been disputed. It is probably no coincidence that by the middle of the 11th century, a successful cult of St Oswald's right arm was being promoted at the reformed Benedictine house of Peterbrough. There may have been other factors which are now entirely beyond our reach.

What is certain is that in (or perhaps a little before) 1033 Cnut used the estates of the new minster as an endowment for his foreign clerk Duduc who soon after became bishop of Wells[27]. Duduc held the estates until his death in 1061, when they seem to have passed into the hands of Archbishop Stigand of Canterbury. After Stigand's deposition in 1070 the estates were used as an endowment for the new Norman archbishop of York, Thomas I. In c.1093 the archbishop obtained the spiritualities as well as the temporalities. In the words of Hamilton Thompson, the appropriation of the new minster to the archbishops of York 'condemned it, throughout its history, to isolation from its natural surroundings and to a somewhat insignificant place among the religious foundations of Gloucestershire'[28].

IV

The materials which I have used in this attempt to reconstruct the pre-Conquest history of the new minster at Gloucester are very diverse. The only document to derive ultimately from its own archive seems to be Athelstan's charter, though some of what William of Malmesbury relates may be based on the muniments of the new minster. But the main reason why we have information about the new minster is its possession of important relics, relics which attracted the attention of writers like William of Malmesbury and like Reginald of Durham who wrote a *Life of St Oswald* in the 1160s. Thus we have to put together the history of the new minster from a range of sources of varying nature, date and quality.

When we come to consider the old minster the position is quite different. Almost all the material that we have derives from its own archives; as previously mentioned, Æthelric's will of 804 is the only document outside its own archive which refers to the old minster before the 1030s. One of the reasons is surely the failure of the old minster ever to promote a successful cult; for instance the old minster has no saint entered in the Old English list of saints' resting-places. This failure continued in the post-Conquest period. In 1524 the last abbot of St Peter's, William Malverne (*alias* Parker), wrote some doggerel verses about the history of the Abbey[29]; when he came to deal with its wonder-working relics, he could do no better than the obscure virgin saint, Arild of Thornbury, on the one hand, and King Edward II on the other hand — hardly an impressive pair.

The principal account of the old minster's history in the pre-Conquest period is the *Historia*, written about 1400 by Abbot Frocester. The *Historia* consists of two parts, first a chronicle which runs from the late 7th century foundation of the Abbey through to Frocester's own day and secondly an index of the properties of the Abbey with an account of how each was acquired; I shall be referring to several entries in the index[30]. In addition there is another version of the Abbey's domestic chronicle in annal form, written by a 13th century monk of Gloucester, Gregory of Caerwent.[31]

The information which these sources provide for the 10th and 11th century history of the old minster is very thin. We cannot even judge whether the old minster maintained adequate records at this period, but we can point to two factors in the post-Conquest period which may have led to a loss of early records. First of all there was damage of some sort in 1088 (see below) and there were fires in 1101 and 1122; of the fire in 1122 it is recorded that 'all the minster was burnt and all the treasures that were there except a few books and three mass vestments'[32]. Secondly it is evident that in the early Norman period the monks of Gloucester Abbey had little interest in their pre-Conquest history; for instance William of Malmesbury, who visited Gloucester, was able to form the opinion that the old minster was founded just before the Norman Conquest[33].

V

We thus have to make a little go a long way in any discussion of the history of the old minster in the 10th and 11th centuries. The first record to be considered is found in the index of properties in the *Historia* . In this entry we are told that in the year 981 'Elfleda, the sister of King Ethelred, gave Hinton to the church of St Peter at Gloucester; she was then barren through age and in dire necessity. And when 5 men were required on the king's service from this little estate and could not be found, the clerks, who then presided over the church of St Peter of Gloucester, came and entreated that lady. Therefore when the king was at his feast on Christmas day, she prostrated herself at his feet, and obtained that the estate might then and thereafter be free and quit'[34]. The main ingredients of this story also occur in Gregory of Caerwent's chronicle, showing that the story was already in existence in the 13th century[35].

This curious story has a number of questionable details. Claims of exemption from military service are often suspicious and we may wonder what sort of document could possibly have preserved the details of Elfleda's sorry state[36]. Moreover if Elfleda were a sister of Æthelred the Unready, her father must have been King Edgar who was himself only born in 943, so Elfleda could hardly have been aged by 981. No sister of Æthelred called Elfleda is known, but there were undoubtedly many royal women in the 10th century, whose names have not survived. It is however worth noting that the Latin *Elfleda* could stand equally for Old English Ælffæd or Æthelflæd[37].

I think that something can perhaps be made of this story if we work on the assumption that it is a story fabricated (as such stories often were) from little more than a list of benefactors and the Domesday Book record that Hinton did not pay geld and was free from all outside service. If we make that assumption then it is striking to note that we could have the names Æthelred and Æthelflæd in conjunction in a Gloucester context. It is tempting to suggest that the original gift was a benefaction of Æthelred and Æthelflæd of Mercia, of whom we have already heard as the founders of the new minster. If so the date of 981 might have been substituted for 891 or 901 or 911.

It is difficult to know precisely how a story of this nature might have evolved, but there is one detail which may tell in favour of this interpretation, namely Elfleda's barren state. William of Malmesbury recounts that Æthelflæd of Mercia abstained from sexual relations after the birth of her first child because 'it was unbecoming the daughter of a king to give way to a delight which, in the course of time, produced such painful consequences'[38]. Perhaps a version of this story became embroiled in Gloucester Abbey's account of the gift of Hinton. It is at any rate an intriguing possibility that Æthelred and Æthelflæd may have been benefactors of the old minster as well as of the new minster.

VI

The next event recorded in the *Historia* is of rather more importance, namely the account of the Benedictine reform which is assigned to the year 1022. The *Historia* tells us that in this year , 'Wulfstan, Bishop of Worcester, afterwards Archbishop of York, with the consent of King Cnut, the leader of the Danes, who exalted the Holy Church and renewed and promoted her ancient liberties, as Peter of Poitiers says; this Wulfstan appointed the clerks, who had previously ruled and guarded the church of St Peter, in the same church according to rule under the protection of the Apostles Peter and Paul and subject to the rule of St Benedict; and he consecrated a certain Edric to be the first abbot and guardian of that house'[39].

There are a number of problems and difficulties in this account. First the chronology is wrong. Wulfstan was archbishop of York from 1002 to 1023, holding Worcester in plurality only until 1016, though it is true that Leofsige, his successor at Worcester, was probably little more than a suffragan at first. Moreover, although Wulfstan himself was probably a monk, he did not leave a reputation elsewhere as a monastic reformer.

Secondly the *Historia* quotes an authority, Peter of Poitiers. The *Historia* does not elsewhere quote its authorities, and it may be a sign that the author knows that he is on uncertain ground. Moreover the authority which is quoted shows the late date of the account contained in the *Historia* . Peter of Poitiers was a master of the school of Paris who died in 1205. He wrote a sacred history which was used in a universal chronicle which became known by his name[40]. The earliest English version dates from the 1240s, and it is thus improbable that the account embodied in the *Historia* originated earlier than the middle of the 13th century.

Thirdly there is no reference to the reform in the other surviving version of the Abbey's domestic chronicle, Gregory of Caerwent; this may well be a significant omission.

Fourthly the account of the reform in the *Historia* is followed by a document which also bears the date 1022. I shall return to that document a little later, but it seems to be the only securely dated document to survive from the archive of the old minster for the period between 862 and 1058. It is of interest to notice that this document does refer to an abbot of the old minster.

What can we make of these difficulties? Abbot Frocester, the author of the *Historia*, would have known from his reading of works such as William of Malmesbury that there certainly should have been a reform in the late Saxon period. It seems to me likely that the account of the reform is no more than an inference on the part of Frocester (or just possibly an earlier chronicler); Frocester probably attached the date of the reform to the one surviving document which he found in his archive, bearing the date 1022 and mentioning an abbot. Frocester made other similar inferences, in particular his apparent belief that religious life ceased after the death of the last abbess in 767, something which we have already seen to be demonstrably wrong.

Gloucester would be by no means exceptional in having preserved no reliable record of the date at which it was reformed. At Worcester a range of different evidence survives, and we know that the process of reform was far more complex than Worcester's later historians would have us believe[41]. The traditions of Bury St Edmunds concerning its purported reform in the reign of Cnut have been demonstrated to be unreliable and probably fictitious[42].

We do not have enough evidence to be certain that Frocester's account is mistaken; it is possible that Gloucester Abbey did preserve a genuine tradition that Wulfstan reformed the old minster. But we are justified in treating the surviving account with considerable suspicion. More positively I think that we can be reasonably sure that the old minster was reformed no later than 1022. Certainly the lease of that date refers to an abbot, while in the 1030s we find the 'community of Gloucester' witnessing a Worcester lease in company with the impeccably monastic communities of Worcester, Evesham and Pershore[43]. We cannot be certain when the old minster was in fact reformed, and in my view a date in the second half of the 10th century is just as likely as a date in the early 11th century.

I want to turn now to the document which follows the account of the Benedictine reform in the *Historia* ; it was probably inserted in the *Historia* to provide support for the preceding passage. This document is in the form of a lease in which Abbot Edric declares that, being compelled by great necessity, he has granted to a certain Stamarcot the lands of Hatherley and of Badgeworth for the term of one life. Edric states that he has done this in consideration of the sum of £15 with which he has redeemed all other lands belonging to the monastery from the great taxation, the heregeld, which was made throughout England[44].

In its present form the lease is in Latin; however it is with little doubt a translation of a document which was originally in Old English[45]. This enables us to explain one feature of the document which has caused earlier students some difficulty, namely the date which is stated to be approximately ('circiter') 1022. But if we work on the basis that the document is a translation from the vernacular, then the date in the original text would probably have been Old English 'ymbe' 1022, a respectable formula found in several contemporary Worcester leases[46].

The lease is a creation of its age, the period immediately after the Danish invasions which resulted in Cnut becoming king of England in 1016. The great heregeld or 'army tax' which troubled Edric so much is almost certainly the immense taxation of £82,500 levied by Cnut in 1018. There is probably another testimony to the effects of that taxation in the Gloucester area in the form of the hoard of coins of Cnut's first issue found at Kingsholm in about 1780[47].

The lands leased by Abbot Edric, Badgeworth and (in all probability) Hatherley, had apparently formed part of the early endowment of the old minster[48]. Although the transaction is stated to be a lease for one life, the old minster never appears to have recovered these lands; according to Domesday Book both Badgeworth and Hatherley were in secular ownership in 1066. Losses of monastic loan-lands were common in the late Saxon period and often seem to have been connected with the tributes and taxations imposed by the Danish kings. The witness list of the lease includes the Danish earl Eilaf, who was related to Cnut by marriage, and it also refers to 'many others both English and Danes'.

To return to abbot Edric, the *Historia* makes him abbot for the whole period from 1022 to 1058[49]. That is probably no more than another inference on the part of Frocester to fill the gap which he is likely to have found until the next event in the records. An abbot called Eadric can be found witnessing an Evesham document dated between 1021 and 1023[50], but if Edric remained abbot of Gloucester until 1058, he witnessed no other surviving charters.

VII

When we come to the next event in the old minster's history, we are fortunate in that we have a much earlier witness than the *Historia* in the form of an entry in the 'D' text of the *Anglo-Saxon Chronicle* for 1058. The exact wording of the entry is important so I will quote the Old English, 'on þam ilcan gere Ealdred biscop halgode þæt mynster on Gleawceastre þe he sylf geforðode Gode to lofe 7 sancte Petre', 'In the same year Bishop Ealdred consecrated the minster at Gloucester which he himself had furthered to the glory of God and St Peter'.

We also have the testimony of many later Latin chronicles which recount that Ealdred rebuilt the church from the foundations. The earliest such chronicle is that of John of Worcester[51], written at Worcester more than 60 years after 1058 and the best part of a generation after Gloucester's present Norman abbey was consecrated in 1100. John of Worcester's own account is likely to be based on the 'D' text or on a similar version of the *Anglo-Saxon Chronicle,* and all the other Latin chronicles derive ultimately from John. That probably includes Gloucester's own *Historia* , which does however add a little additional information[52].

The 'D' text of the *Anglo-Saxon Chronicle* does not in fact say that Ealdred rebuilt the old minster entirely, for the annalist does not use the Old English verb 'timbrian', 'to build'; rather he uses the verb 'geforðian', which is the root of the modern verb 'to further'[53].

It is a dangerous business using linguistic niceties in a discussion of architectural history, particularly at a period when the language did not contain a sophisticated architectural vocabulary. However I think that the 'D' text annal may mean something different to a

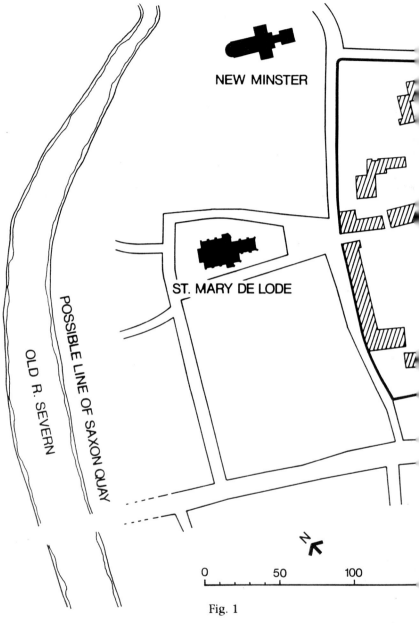

NEW MINSTER

ST. MARY DE LODE

POSSIBLE LINE OF SAXON QUAY

OLD R. SEVERN

0   50   100

Fig. 1

Plan of the north-west quarter of Glou[
of the Anglo-Saxon old minster. The wal
by a solid black line; the Roman wall i
Moss.

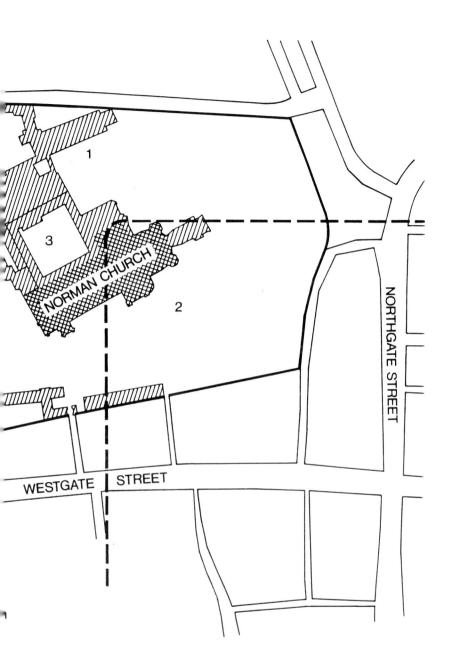

1

3

NORMAN CHURCH

2

NORTHGATE STREET

WESTGATE STREET

to show the possible sites (1, 2 and 3)
e medieval Abbey precincts is indicated
cated by a broken line. Drawn by Phil

complete rebuilding. In last year's lecture Patrick Wormald stressed the prominence of Ealdred in the 'D' text in the middle years of the 11th century[54]. In all likelihood the annalist was closely associated with Ealdred, and the annalist may well have known exactly what Ealdred's works at Gloucester entailed. While the wording of the annal does not exclude the possibility that Ealdred rebuilt the old minster, it does also permit other interpretations, for instance that the old minster was remodelled or refurbished or subjected to what we would today call a liturgical reordering.

A remodelling is perhaps what we might expect from our knowledge of other Anglo-Saxon church buildings. Richard Gem has recently written of 'the principle that the first buildings on the site seem to have become normative for all the subsequent developments, perhaps because they were regarded as relics of their saintly founders. The consequence of this was that the churches were never replanned and rebuilt when needs and fashions changed; rather they acquired new elements that were grafted onto the old to form an organic whole'[55]. Richard Gem was writing about St Augustine's at Canterbury, Glastonbury and the Old Minster at Winchester. However the principle is applicable here at Deerhurst too; the many changes which the building underwent before the Norman Conquest all respected the central rectangle in which you are sitting. Total rebuildings were rare in the Anglo-Saxon period, and I see no reason why the old minster at Gloucester should have been an exception.

I want now to indulge in some mild speculations about why Ealdred rebuilt or, as I have suggested, remodelled the old minster at Gloucester. Ealdred's career began as a monk of the Old Minster at Winchester. He became abbot of Tavistock in 1027 and bishop of Worcester in 1046; it was as bishop of Worcester that he consecrated Odda's chapel at Deerhurst in April 1056. In 1061 he was appointed archbishop of York and it was Ealdred who crowned both Harold and William the Conqueror in 1066. He died three years later in 1069. His career included several important diplomatic missions abroad, including a visit of about a year to Cologne in 1054[56].

I do not think that it is primarily in his capacity as diocesan bishop that Ealdred rebuilt or remodelled the old minster at Gloucester. It is true that when Ealdred was archbishop of York, he did carry out works at Beverley and Southwell. Beverley and Southwell were however episcopal minsters important for the administration of the huge northern see of York. There is no suggestion in either Gloucester or Worcester sources that Gloucester ever played a similar role in the diocese of Worcester.

Recent research has focussed attention on a different aspect of Ealdred's career, his role as a reformer of church liturgy and ceremonial, particularly royal ceremonial[57]. He was responsible for the introduction of the Romano-German Pontifical to England, and he probably wrote the third English coronation *ordo* for use in 1066. Most importantly for present purposes, he introduced to England from Germany the *laudes regiae,* the royal acclamations. Ealdred's visit to Germany in 1054 must have been crucial in these developments.

The obituary notice for William the Conqueror (1066-1087) in the *Anglo-Saxon Chronicle* includes the well-known statement that 'three times every year he wore his crown, as often as he was in England. At Easter he wore it at Winchester, at Whitsuntide at Westminster and at Christmas at Gloucester'. We know of only three years in the later part of William's reign when he actually did celebrate Christmas at Gloucester, though there are gaps in his itinerary and he was sometimes in Normandy. It is however clear that Gloucester was a major ceremonial centre at least in the later part of William's reign. Ritual crown-wearings such as those described in the *Anglo-Saxon Chronicle* had both festive and ecclesiastical aspects. The involvement of Gloucester Abbey in the crown-wearings of William I and of William II (1087-1100) is made clear by a writ of Henry I issued in 1100 in favour of the monks of Westminster, Winchester and Gloucester[58]. It must have been in the church rebuilt or remodelled by Ealdred that William the Conqueror wore his crown when he celebrated Christmas at Gloucester.

The question which arises is thus as follows. Was Gloucester already a royal ceremonial centre in the reign of Edward the Confessor and was it primarily as a royal ceremonial church that Ealdred rebuilt or remodelled the old minster at Gloucester? It is a question that can only be answered with great caution.

It is certain that Gloucester had once again become the focus of royal attention in the generation before the Conquest. Harthacnut visited Gloucester at least once, but it is during Edward the Confessor's reign (1042-1066) that Gloucester returned to prominence. Gloucester features regularly in Edward's itinerary with eight recorded visits, a number surpassed only by Edward's own favoured residence at Westminster[59].

There is however no distinct pattern of seasonal residence at the three centres of Winchester, Westminster and Gloucester during Edward the Confessor's reign, though he was at Gloucester at Christmas in 1052 and in 1062 and at Easter in 1058 and perhaps 1062. Attempts by an earlier generation of scholars to show that ritual crown-wearing existed before the Norman Conquest have not stood the test of rigorous examination, and the earliest text of the *laudes regiae* introduced by Ealdred was prepared for use no earlier than the coronation of the Conqueror's queen, Mathilda, at Whitsun 1068.

Despite the lack of evidence, most scholars would allow the possibility that such ritual may already have been developing in Edward the Confessor's reign under the auspices of Ealdred, particularly after his visit to Cologne in 1054. Our question cannot be answered with certainty, but it is a strong and intriguing possibility that Ealdred's main purpose in rebuilding or remodelling the old minster at Gloucester was to provide an appropriate setting for royal ceremonial.

Ealdred would have seen many recent building projects in Germany. If we look for an inspiration for his work at Gloucester, it is perhaps to be found in the minster church ('Cathedral') of St Simon and St Jude at Goslar, which was specially built for crown-wearing by the Emperor Henry III (1039-1056) and which was consecrated in 1051 by Archbishop Herimann II of Cologne, Ealdred's host in 1054. Ealdred may well have visited Goslar, for Henry III celebrated Christmas there in 1054. The most striking feature of the minster at Goslar was a splendid, though old-fashioned, westwork. Ealdred's work at Gloucester perhaps included a similar feature.

The points which I have discussed do have some relevance to the existing building of Gloucester Cathedral, for it has sometimes been suggested that part of Ealdred's building survives in the crypt. The balance of opinion is now strongly against this view. If Ealdred's church is our main perspective, we can add two further arguments to the weight of opinion in favour of the crypt having been begun by Abbot Serlo in 1089. First, if Ealdred merely remodelled the old minster and did not rebuild it, as I have suggested, then it is improbable that any part of a traditional building of the Anglo-Saxon period would be incorporated in the Norman Abbey church begun in 1089. Secondly we know that Ealdred's interests and contacts were with Germany rather than with Normandy; at Beverley the new screen built by Ealdred is specifically stated to have been of German workmanship (*opere Theutonico*). Art historians seem to be agreed on the Norman character of the crypt at Gloucester[60], and on this basis I see nothing to suggest work likely to have been carried out by Ealdred.

Although none of Ealdred's church appears to survive, a little can perhaps be said about its decoration. It may have had an inscription, perhaps similar to the inscription commemorating Ealdred's conse-cration of Odda's chapel at Deerhurst in 1056. Something like an inscription is probably the source of the information provided by the *Historia* (and not by any other source) that Ealdred consecrated the old minster on 15 October 1058[61].

More interestingly Ealdred's church may have had a major statue. In his seminal paper on Ealdred's liturgical interests, Michael Lapidge discussed a small collection of documents which he showed to have an intimate association with Ealdred. One of these documents was a blessing for a statue of St Peter, and Lapidge suggested that 'Ealdred, who was ever a man for lavish display, could well have donated funds for a statue of St Peter at the church of St Peter in Gloucester built by him'[62]. Ealdred did in fact have connections with quite a number of churches dedicated to St Peter, not least the church of his archiepis-copal see at York, but equally he may well have commissioned more than one image of St Peter.

Daglingworth Church, Gloucestershire: statue of St Peter. Photo: Mick Sharp

There are few surviving large-scale images of St Peter from Anglo-Saxon England. There is however a statue of him at Daglingworth in Gloucestershire (Fig 2), probably belonging to the second half of the 11th century or even the early 12th century. Whatever the exact date of the sculpture, it is a traditional Anglo-Saxon representation of St Peter, beardless and tonsured[63]. It is pleasant to reflect that at Daglingworth we may possibly have a rustic reflection of a major image of St Peter at Gloucester commissioned by Ealdred.

There is one possible surviving sculpture from Ealdred's church, a damaged stone roundel of Christ found in the early years of this century in the garden wall of the Bishop's Palace. However the opinion of art-historians as to the date of this piece ranges from the mid-10th century to the mid-12th century[64].

The scale of Ealdred's works at Gloucester should not lightly be under-estimated. Ealdred acquired control of three of Gloucester's manors, something which led to a dispute which lasted until 1157 between Gloucester Abbey and the see of York, to which Ealdred had transferred the manors. Prior David of Worcester, giving evidence in this dispute in the middle of the 12th century, recounted that Ealdred acquired control of these manors specifically on account of his construction works[65]. If Prior David's statement is accepted, then the value of the manors concerned indicates work on a substantial scale. Indeed Ealdred seems to have acquired the plums among the old minster's estates, at least if the evidence of Domesday Book is taken at face value. In 1066 the three manors held by Ealdred were rated at 49 hides and had a value of £39; the remaining estates of the old minster in Gloucestershire were rated at 86 hides, but had a value of only £36.

Ealdred also appointed the last Anglo-Saxon abbot of Gloucester, Wilstan, a monk of Worcester. According to Prior David's evidence, Wilstan was a kinsman of Ealdred[66]. Quite a lot is known about Wilstan's career at Worcester. He had been a monk there for more than 40 years when he was appointed to Gloucester; he first appears as a deacon in 1016. In the mid-1050s he was *praepositus* (sub-prior) at the time that St Wulfstan was prior of Worcester. In the pages of Hemming we find Wulfstan and Wilstan acting together to recover lands lost to the see of Worcester, for instance on the death-bed of Godwin, the brother of Earl Leofric. Wilstan cannot have been a young man when he was appointed to Gloucester in 1058, and he must have been elderly by 1072 when he died on pilgrimage to Jerusalem[67].

VIII

Ealdred's church did not survive for long. Serlo, the first Norman abbot, began the construction of the new Abbey church in 1089 and it was consecrated in 1100[68]. There are some clues as to the fate of Ealdred's church. The property index in the *Historia* contains an entry relating to the gift of lands in Wales by Bernard of Neufmarché in 1088. At the end of this entry we find the following statement, 'In this year Gloucester and the church of St Peter were destroyed on account of the war between the magnates of England' *(Hoc anno propter werram motam inter primates Angliae destructa est Gloucestria et ecclesia Sancti Petri)*[69]. In its present place this statement makes no sense. However, as Christopher Brooke has pointed out, what seems to have happened here is that an entry from the Abbey's chronicle for 1088 has been moved bodily into the index as a result of the incompetence of the scribe[70]. Moreover the destruction of 1088 seems to be followed logically by the start made on the new Norman church in 1089.

It may, however, be doubted whether the destruction of 1088 was quite as complete as might appear at first sight. The account of the destruction does not seem to have enjoyed a prominent position in the Abbey's chronicle entry for 1088[71]. The destruction is not recorded in any of the other sources dealing with the civil war of 1088, as we might fairly expect that it would have been if the Abbey church had been destroyed beyond repair. Moreover, a great deal happened at Gloucester before the dedication of the Norman abbey church in 1100, and some of what happened seems to imply the existence of a major church at Gloucester. The 19th century historian, Professor Freeman, wrote that 'It was in Gloucester, more than in any other place, that the Red King gathered his assemblies and showed his pride of kingship'[72]. William Rufus (1087-1100) celebrated Christmas at Gloucester on at least two occasions[73]; as Henry

I's writ indicates, William presumably wore his crown as his father had before him. It was probably in the Anglo-Saxon old minster that Anselm was proclaimed archbishop amid extraordinary scenes on 6 March 1093[74].

It is not difficult to reconcile these various points, for monastic chroniclers were much given to exaggerating reports of destruction by fire and by war. What probably happened was that the old minster suffered some damage in 1088 but was not destroyed. In all likelihood it remained in use until the new Norman Abbey church was consecrated on 15 July 1100 and was pulled down soon afterwards.

IX

Much of what I have said about the old minster, in particular about its history over the last 40 years or so of its life, is capable of being tested by archaeology. It is, therefore, desirable to give thought as to where it may have stood. Some initial assumptions can be made:-

1. It is likely to have stood somewhere within the Abbey precincts (Fig 1).

2. The church of St Peter was probably only one of a group of churches comprising the 'old minster' in the early medieval period[75].

3. We can be reasonably confident that, at least in its later phases, the old minster is likely to have been a stone building.

4. The Norman Abbey church shows some concern for proper orientation, a concern often found in major Romanesque churches in England. Unlike the Norman Abbey, the Anglo-Saxon buildings probably respected the alignment of the Roman town.

I think that we can identify three main possible sites for the old minster church of St Peter (Fig 1):-

1. The area of the Abbey infirmary. This area was favoured by Early Modern antiquaries, who believed that the pre-Conquest buildings survived to a late date (the views of one antiquary, Prebendary

William Loe, are explored in more detail in the Appendix). Though I do not consider it likely, it is just possible that this opinion is based on a medieval tradition which has some basis in reality[76].

2. The north-west corner of the Roman town. This position has been favoured by most recent students, and this view has much to commend it. However, the relationship between the walled town and its western suburb is not well understood. For instance, dates as far apart as the 4th and late 11th centuries have been proposed for the demolition of the Roman west wall.

3. The third possibility is that the Anglo-Saxon buildings lay to the west of the Roman wall and ditch, perhaps somewhere close to or under the present nave, in a position similar to that of the Old Minster at Winchester[77]. In this position the old minster of St Peter could be seen in conjunction with the church of St Mary de Lode; St Mary de Lode was the parish church which served the Abbey's estates near Gloucester in the 12th century and it seems to have been of ancient, if obscure, origin[78]. Early medieval church groups commonly included buildings planned in a linear arrangement with dedications to St Peter and to St Mary[79]. An interesting parallel may be noted in Bath (the other foundation of Osric in the late 7th century); the church of St Mary de Stalls apparently stood a little to the west of the main abbey church of St Peter[80]. This third position is my own favoured option. If I had free use of the trowel, or even of the ground penetrating radar now so successfully operated by the Gloucester City Excavation Unit, it is under the present cloisters that I would first look.[81]

X (Summary)

There is an enormous amount that we do not know about the ecclesiastical history of Gloucester in the 10th and 11th centuries. Although I have suggested that the new minster may have played a role in the programme of educational reform instigated by King Alfred, we can say almost nothing with confidence about the role of either minster in the cultural life of the age[82]. For a period of about a century from the 920s, we have no records of any kind. At the end of this century there had evidently been a major shift in the pattern of royal patronage.

By the mid-11th century the new minster was a house of secular canons, valued primarily for the use to which its endowments could be put by the king; it was destined to become an Augstinian priory of minor significance. It is an enduring mystery why a house possessing relics of the greatest royal saint of Anglo-Saxon England became such a spectacular failure.

By contrast the old minster was a reformed Benedictine abbey which had retained much of its early endowments for its own use, and at a date close to the Norman Conquest it became a royal ceremonial church. It could hardly fail to flourish as one of the great abbeys of the kingdom, even though its failure to promote a successful cult meant that it would never rank alongside houses such as Durham or Glastonbury.

APPENDIX

The historical tract known as the 'Memoriale Ecclesiae Cathedralis Gloucestriae Compendiarum' has long been known to Gloucester historians, for it was printed by Sir William Dugdale in the *Monasticon Anglicanum* in 1655 (vol 1, p 993) from a manuscript in the custody of the Dean and Chapter of Gloucester when Dugdale saw it. This manuscript was in the hands of Anthony Wood by 1661 and is now Oxford, Bodleian Library, MS. Wood B.1. (S.C. 8572). The tract provides a history of Gloucester Abbey and Cathedral from an anti-monastic viewpoint. The manuscript bears the date 1608 and the text takes the history of the Cathedral down to 1607 (Dugdale did not print the section concerned with the period after the Reformation; this section does little more than describe the succession of bishops and deans). The manuscript is anonymous, but on the basis of the handwriting, the author can be identified as Prebendary William Loe, a Puritan cleric of Gloucester Cathedral from 1602[83] (the identification of Loe as the author is based on a comparison of Wood B.1. with the accounts for 1609-10 prepared by Loe for the Dean and Chapter of Gloucester, now Gloucester Record Office, D936A1/1, pp. 1-17).

The anonymous publication of Loe's tract in the *Monasticon* has given it a spurious authority which has misled many of Gloucester's historians. In particular one statement by Loe has bedevilled discussions of Gloucester's early medieval topography, his claim that Ealdred rebuilt the Abbey church 'a little further from the place where it had stood before and nearer to the side of the town' *(a loco quo prius steterat paulo remotius et urbis lateri magis contiguum).* It is, however, difficult to believe that Loe, writing 450 years after the event, had access to a source which accurately described Ealdred's work in 1058, particularly as Loe is much given to flights of fancy; if Loe did have access to such a source, it was apparently ignored by Gloucester's medieval historians such as Frocester. The source, if it existed, does not seem to have provided any other early medieval material. Moreover Loe's topographical knowledge seems to be based entirely on what could be seen in the early 17th century.

At a later point in the tract, Loe refers to a stained glass window in the east walk of the cloister which purported to depict the Anglo-Saxon church in the time of the nuns (the window was destroyed later in the 17th century; as Abbot Frocester built the cloisters this stained glass window is thus likely to be another aspect of the historical interest which produced the *Historia*). Loe interpreted the window as showing the early church close to the infirmary and it seems probable that Loe's opinions about the whereabouts of the early medieval buildings were based on this stained glass window or on some similar visual source.

Loe's version of the history of Gloucester Abbey merits further study. However, no trust can be placed in his statement about Ealdred's church, and unless evidence can be found to support it, it should be discounted in future discussions of Gloucester's early medieval topography.

Acknowledgements

I am grateful to all those who have discussed aspects of Gloucester's ecclesiastical history with me. In particular I would like to thank John Blair, Richard Bryant, Richard Gem, Carolyn Heighway, Dick Holt, Simon Keynes, David Parsons and Alex Rumble. Patrick Wormald kindly allowed me to see a draft of his Deerhurst lecture in advance of publication. The text was typed by Anne Sadler.

FOOTNOTES

The text printed here is a slightly expanded version of the lecture given on 3rd October 1992. I have not attempted to provide full references for every statement for reasons of space, and a more detailed discussion of the evidence for the new minster (St Oswald's) will be found in Hare, forthcoming. In the meantime reference may be made to Carolyn Heighway's interim excavation reports in vols. 58 (1978) and 60 (1980) of the *Antiquaries Journal*. I also hope to be able to elaborate further the discussion of the old minster in future papers.

The following abbreviations are used in the footnotes:-

Cart. Glos.　　　　　　　W H Hart (ed), *Historia et Cartularium Monasterii Sancti Petri Gloucestriae* (Rolls Series, 3 vols, 1863-7)

Hare, forthcoming　　　M J Hare, 'The documentary evidence' in C M Heighway and R M Bryant, *The Saxon Minster and Medieval Priory of St Oswald at Gloucester*, in preparation.

S　　　　　　　　　　　P H Sawyer, *Anglo-Saxon Charters: an Annotated List and Bibliography* (1968)

WMGP　　　　　　　　N E S A Hamilton (ed), *Willelmi Malmesbiriensis Monachi De Gestis Pontificum Anglorum* (Rolls Series, 1870)

WMGR　　　　　　　　W Stubbs (ed), *Willelmi Malmesbiriensis Monachi De Gestis Regum Anglorum* (Rolls Series, 2 vols, 1887-9)

1.　The detailed evidence for the dedications and other names of the two minsters will be set out in Hare, forthcoming.
2.　H P R Finberg, *The Early Charters of the West Midlands* (2nd ed, 1972), 153-166.
3.　*Cart. Glos.* i, 7.
4.　S 1187.
5.　P Wormald, *How do we know so much about Anglo-Saxon Deerhurst?*, Deerhurst Lecture 1991 (1993), 2-7.
6.　*Cart. Glos.* i, 5. I am grateful to Dr Veronica Ortenberg for discussing the early development of the cult of St Petronilla with me.

7. For detailed references to what follows see S Keynes and M Lapidge, *Alfred the Great*, 1983, passim.
8. A T Thacker, 'Chester and Gloucester: Early Ecclesiastical Organization in two Midland burhs', *Northern History* 18 (1982), 199-211 at 211.
9. S 223.
10. WMGP, 293.
11. For Winchester see M Biddle (ed), *Winchester in the Early Middle Ages* (Winchester Studies, vol. 1), 1976, 313-321.
12. For the site of the Kingsholm palace see C M Heighway, 'Excavations at Gloucester', *Antiquaries Journal* 58 (1978), 103-132, Fig. 1.
13. Keynes and Lapidge, *op. cit.*, 26.
14. D Dumville, *Wessex and England from Alfred to Edgar*, 1992, chapters 3-6.
15. WMGR, ii, 133.
16. S 223.
17. Finberg, *loc. cit.* in note 1. However, Professor Nicholas Brooks tells me that he believes that much of what Finberg considered to be 9th century material is likely to be of 12th century origin; he hopes to prepare a paper on the early history of the Gloucester old minster.
18. C Johnson and H A Cronne (eds), *Regesta Regum Anglo-Normannorum*, ii, no. 1936.
19. Thacker, *op.cit.*
20. Athelstan's charter was quoted by the prior of St Oswald's in an early-14th century court case, printed in G O Sayles (ed), *Select Cases in the Court of King's Bench under Edward I*, vol. 3, 1939, no. 76, pp. 138-144. Dr Simon Keynes and Dr Alex Rumble have both provided helpful advice about this document.
21. For the importance of Oswald to the West Saxon royal house see J L Nelson, 'Reconstructing a royal family: reflections on Alfred' in I Wood and N Lund (eds), *People and places in northern Europe, 500-1600: essays in honour of Peter Hayes Sawyer*, 1991, 47-66, at 52-3.
22. Hare, forthcoming.
23. Wormald, *op. cit.*, 7-9.
24. WMGP, 293.
25. *Cart. Glos.* i, 8-9.
26. I owe this point to Dr Alex Rumble.
27. The detailed evidence for the 11th century history of the new minster will be set out in Hare, forthcoming.
28. A H Thompson, 'The jurisdiction of the archbishops of York in Gloucestershire', *Transactions of the Bristol and Gloucestershire Archaeological Society*, 43 (1921), 85-180, at 129.

29. William Malverne's verses were printed by T Hearne (ed), *Robert of Gloucester's Chronicle*, vol. 2, 1714, 578-585.
30. The *Historia* is printed in *Cart. Glos.* i, 3-125. There is a valuable study of the genesis of the *Historia* in C N L Brooke, *The Church and the Welsh Border in the Central Middle Ages*, 1986, 50-70.
31. Gregory of Caewent's Chronicle was excerpted in the 16th century by Laurence Nowell; Nowell's excerpts survive in London, British Library, MS. Cotton Vespasian A.v., fols. 195r-203v. I hope to produce an edition of this text.
32. C Clark (ed), *The Peterborough Chronicle, 1070-1154*, 1958, *s.a.* 1122.
33. WMGR, ii, 136; WMGP, 292.
34. *Cart. Glos.* i, 87.
35. However, the reference to clerks is not found in Gregory, a point relevant to the discussion of the Benedictine reform.
36. I owe this point to Dr Simon Keynes (pers. comm. dated 25 May 1986).
37. William of Malmesbury uses the form 'Elfleda' for the Lady Æthelflæd of the Mercians; WMGP, 293.
38. WMGR, ii, 136.
39. *Cart. Glos.* i, 8.
40. P S Moore, *The Works of Peter of Poitiers*, Catholic University of America, 1956, 111-117; a preliminary look at some of the chronicles known by the name of Peter of Poitiers has not revealed any exact verbal connection with the Gloucester *Historia*.
41. Several papers at the St Oswald Millennium Conference at Worcester in September 1992 shed new light on the reform at Worcester; the proceedings are expected to appear in a volume being edited by Professor Nicholas Brooks.
42. A Gransden, 'The legends and traditions concerning the origins of the Abbey of Bury St Edmunds', *English Historical Review*, 100 (1985), 1-24. If the thesis put forward in this lecture is accepted, no Benedictine foundations can now be reliably assigned to the reign of Cnut (1016-1035).
43. S 1399.
44. *Cart. Glos.* i, 8-9 (S 1424).
45. I owe this point to Dr Alex Rumble.
46. For instance S 1309, S 1326 and S 1332.
47. R H M Dolley and D M Metcalf, 'Cnut's Quatrefoil type in English cabinets of the eighteenth century', *British Numismatic Journal*, 29 (1958/9), 69-81.

48. *Cart. Glos.* i, 1xxii. Hatherley is adjacent to and may originally have been part of Badgeworth.
49. *Cart. Glos.* i, 8.
50. S 977. In this lecture I have not discussed the gift of Churcham, assigned to Edric's abbacy (*Cart. Glos.* i, 67-68).
51. B Thorpe (ed), *Florentii Wigorniensis Monachi Chronicon ex Chronicis* (1848-9), i, 217.
52. For connections between the Gloucester chronicle and John of Worcester, see Brooke, *op. cit.*, 65-66.
53. The same annalist does use the verb 'timbrian' elsewhere; it occurs twice in the 1055 annal.
54. Wormald, *op. cit.*, 9-17.
55. R D H Gem in N Ramsay, M Sparks and T Tatton-Brown (eds), *St Dunstan: his life, times and cult*, 1992, 57-73, at 71.
56. For Ealdred's career see J M Cooper, *The last four Anglo-Saxon Archbishops of York* (Borthwick papers no. 38, 1970), 23-29.
57. For Ealdred's liturgical interests the following papers are essential: H E J Cowdrey, 'The Anglo-Norman *Laudes Regiae*', *Viator* 12 (1981), 39-78; M Lapidge, 'Ealdred of York and MS Cotton Vitellius E. XII', *Yorkshire Archaeological Journal* 55 (1983), 11-25; M Biddle, 'Seasonal Festivals and Residence: Winchester, Westminster and Gloucester in the Tenth to Twelfth Centuries', *Anglo-Norman Studies* 8 (1986), 51-72; J Nelson, 'The Rites of the Conqueror' in J Nelson, *Politics and Ritual in Early Medieval Europe*, 1986, 371-401.
58. Johnson and Cronne, *op. cit.*, no. 490.
59. For Edward's itinerary see T J Oleson, *The Witenagemot in the Reign of Edward the Confessor*, Toronto, 1955, Appendix T, 170-171. It is tempting to suggest that Gloucester's return to prominence at this time is partly explained by the fact that it was a traditional royal centre within the diocese held by Ealdred.
60. See for instance E Fernie, *The Architecture of the Anglo-Saxons*, 1983, 160.
61. *Cart. Glos.* i, 9.
62. Lapidge, *op. cit.*, 20.
63. J Higgitt, 'The Iconography of St Peter in Anglo-Saxon England, and St Cuthbert's Coffin' in G Bonner, D Rollason & C Stancliffe (eds), *St Cuthbert, his cult and his community to AD 1200*, 1989, 267-285.
64. D Welander, *The History, Art and Architecture of Gloucester Cathedral*, 1991, 12-13.
65. *Cart. Glos.* ii, 115.
66. ibid.
67. *Cart. Glos.* i, 9. The career of Wilstan is most easily traced by reference

to I Atkins, 'The Church of Worcester from the Eighth Century to the Twelfth Century, Part II', *Antiquaries Journal* 20 (1940), 1-38.

68. *Cart. Glos.* i, 11-12.
69. *Cart. Glos.* i, 80.
70. Brooke, *op. cit.*, 53-54.
71. The destruction of 1088 is not recorded either in the chronicle in the *Historia* or in Gregory of Caerwent.
72. E A Freeman, 'Gloucester: Its Abbey and Cathedral, and their place in English History', *Records of Gloucester Cathedral* 1 (1882-3), 18-37, at 33.
73. Biddle, *op. cit.*, Appendix B.
74. M Rule (ed), *Eadmeri Historia Novorum in Anglia* (Rolls Series, 1884), 360. Eadmer simply says that Anselm was carried 'in vicinam ecclesiam' which could perhaps refer to a chapel at Kingsholm.
75. J Blair, 'Anglo-Saxon minsters: a topographical review' in J Blair and R Sharpe (eds), *Pastoral Care Before the Parish*, 1992, 226-266, esp. 246-258.
76. Leland appears to have believed that Osric's 7th century church was still standing in the 16th century: T Hearne (ed), *Joannis Lelandi Antiquarii de Rebus Britannicis Collectanea*, 1715, iii, 159.
77. See Martin Biddle's plan in D Parsons (ed), *Tenth-Century Studies*, 1975, 131.
78. For St Mary de Lode see the (slightly divergent) views of Steve Bassett and John Blair, both in Blair and Sharpe, *op. cit.*, 26-29 and 242.
79. Blair cites several examples, *loc. cit.* in note 75.
80. B Cunliffe, 'Saxon Bath' in J Haslam (ed), *Anglo-Saxon Towns in Southern England*, 1984, 345-358, Figs. 115 & 116.
81. The archaeological interest of the cloisters was enhanced in 1980 when observation of a mechanical excavation revealed early medieval burials, together with traces of buildings on a different alignment to that of the present cloisters: A P Garrod and C M Heighway, *Garrod's Gloucester: Archaeological Observations 1974-81*, 1984, 53-55.
82. There were three books of pre-Conquest date at Gloucester in the later medieval period, but none were certainly there before 1066. The books in question are: Gloucester, Dean and Chapter MS. 35 and London, British Library, MSS. Royal 5 A.XI (fols. 47-92) and Royal 13 C.V.
83. For Loe's career see J N Langston, 'Headmasters and Ushers of the King's (College) School, Gloucester, 1541-1841', *Records of Gloucester Cathedral* 3 (part 2, 1927), 159-172.